Understanding Diseases and Disorders

Leprosy

Rachel Lynette

KIDHAVEN PRESS

An imprint of Thomson Gale, a part of The Thomson Corporation

THOMSON
™
GALE

Detroit • New York • San Francisco • San Diego • New Haven, Conn. • Waterville, Maine • London • Munich

For more information, contact
KidHaven Press
27500 Drake Rd.
Farmington Hills, MI 48331-3535
Or you can visit our Internet site at http://www.gale.com

LIBRARY OF CONGRESS CATALOGING-IN-PUBLICATION DATA

Lynette, Rachel.
  Leprosy / by Rachel Lynette.
    p. cm. — (Understanding diseases and disorders)
  Includes bibliographical references and index.
  Contents: Leprosy: A terrifying disease—What causes leprosy?—Living with leprosy—Leprosy today.
  ISBN 0-7377-3172-9 (hardcover : alk. paper)
  1. Leprosy—Juvenile literature. I. Title. II. Series.
  RC154L96 2005
  616.9'98—dc22
                                        2005012168

Printed in the United States of America

Contents

Chapter One

Leprosy: A Terrifying Disease

L eprosy (often called Hansen's disease) is one of the oldest and most feared diseases in history. It is a bacterial disease that commonly attacks the skin, nerves, eyes, and nose. Leprosy can cause permanent nerve damage and severe **deformities**. These deformities make it impossible for people who have leprosy to hide the disease.

Until recently, no one knew what caused leprosy or how to cure it. People with leprosy were called lepers and treated as outcasts. People avoided lepers because they thought lepers were evil and because they were afraid of catching the disease.

The history of leprosy is a sad one, but today leprosy can be treated and cured. Medical professionals know that although leprosy is a **contagious** disease, about 95 percent of the population is naturally immune to it. This means that if they are exposed to the disease their bodies will fight it off and they will not get sick.

Leprosy strikes people of all ages, but some people are more likely to get it than others. For example, children seem to be more susceptible to the disease, and men get leprosy more often than women. Leprosy is also more common in underdeveloped countries. This may be because poor sanitation and crowded living conditions help to spread the disease.

The knowledge of how leprosy is spread and how it can be cured has taken away the **stigma** associated with the disease. People do not fear the disease as much as they did in the past. In most parts

A leprosy patient with severe deformities on his arms and hands lies in a bed at a hospital in the Philippines.

of the world, people who have leprosy are no longer treated as outcasts even though many of their symptoms are visible to others.

Effects of Leprosy

Leprosy affects people in several ways. The word *leprosy* comes from the Greek word *lepros*, which means "scaly." People with leprosy do not actually develop scales, but the disease does attack the skin. It also attacks the nerves, hands, and feet as well as the eyes and the inside of the nose. In some cases, it can also attack muscle and bone. Leprosy develops slowly over a period of years.

The first signs of leprosy are **lesions** on the skin. Lesions are oddly shaped red patches. As the lesions grow into raised bumps, they change in color, becoming darker around the edges and pale in the center. The person will feel **numbness** wherever there is a lesion.

Leprosy also attacks the nerves in the hands and feet. The first signs will be numbness in the toes and fingers. This loss of sensation may result in people damaging those parts of their body further because they do not know they are in danger. For example, people with leprosy may get burned on a hot stove because they cannot feel the heat and do not jerk their hand away. Or they might step on something sharp and ignore the injury because they cannot feel the pain. There have even been cases of people whose fingers and toes have been chewed on by rats while they slept.

In 1989, Princess Diana visited young leprosy patients in Indonesia. Children are more susceptible to the disease than adults.

These injuries often become infected, causing more damage. For example, severe infections can lead to **gangrene**. This means that the tissues in that part of the body die and rot. This can cause the affected area to turn black, become deformed, and produce an unpleasant odor. Gangrene is not curable and the affected part of the body may have to

Leprosy: A Terrifying Disease   7

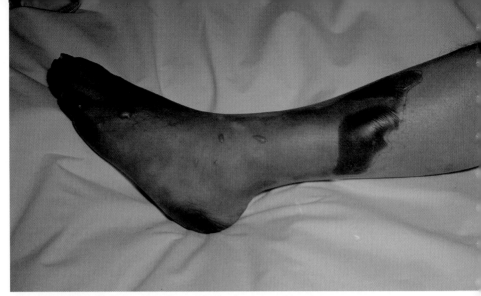

The blackened areas of this patient's foot and leg are infected with gangrene.

be **amputated** to keep the infection from spreading.

People with leprosy may also lose their ability to use their hands and feet. As the disease attacks the nerves, the person may become **paralyzed** in that part of their body. This can result in a condition called "dropped foot" or "dropped wrist" in which the hand or foot hangs limply. Claw hand is also common. As the nerves die, the fingers of the hand curl into a claw and the person is unable to uncurl them.

When leprosy attacks the face, it can result in damage to the eyes. For example, leprosy can cause numbness and paralysis in the eyes. If the eyelid is paralyzed, the person will not be able to blink to avoid getting particles such as sand or dirt in his eyes. When particles do get in the eye, often the person cannot feel them and will not try to remove them. Another problem is that if the eye cannot blink, it cannot moisten itself. And dry eyes result in infections. Infections can then cause the eye to develop ulcers and scar tissue, which can cause blindness.

Leprosy can also damage a person's nose. When leprosy attacks the mucous membranes in the nose, it can harm the nasal passages. At first, the person will have a chronically stuffy nose, but eventually the disease can damage the cartilage in the nose, causing both nostrils to collapse.

Other effects of leprosy include dry skin, loss of hair and nails, muscle weakness, thickening of the skin, the inability to sweat, and **disfiguring** lumps.

A doctor examines the face of a leprosy patient whose nose has been damaged by the disease.

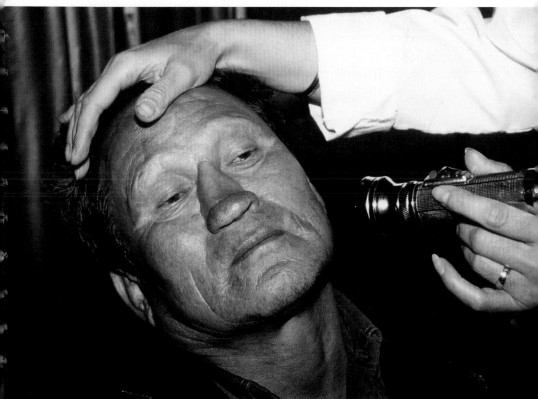

While not as serious as some of the other effects of leprosy, these conditions add to the person's discomfort.

People rarely die from leprosy, but they do sometimes die from complications of the disease. For example, a person with leprosy who cannot work because of the disability might die from malnutrition or from injuries that have become infected. The disease may also weaken a person's immune system, making him or her more likely to get other diseases, such as human immunodeficiency virus (HIV) or pneumonia.

Spread of Leprosy

No one knows exactly when leprosy began, but scientists have theories where it began. Most believe that leprosy began in the East and spread westward. Ancient writings from China and India contain descriptions of a disease that might have been leprosy. Signs of leprosy have even been found in the remains of mummies from ancient Egypt, and the *Bible* has many references to leprosy. The disease was most likely spread throughout Asia and Africa by travelers and traders.

Christian crusaders who left Europe in hopes of capturing the city of Jerusalem probably brought leprosy back to Europe on their return trip home. There were four Crusades between 1095 and 1272. Although the crusaders failed to take Jerusalem, they did manage to spread leprosy to the many towns and villages

The Spread of Leprosy

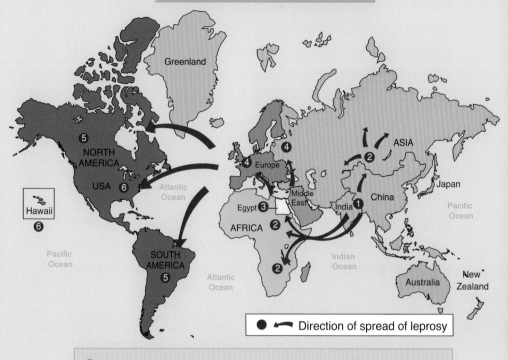

❶ Scientists speculate that leprosy began in ancient China and India and spread to the West. ❷ Ancient travelers and traders spread the disease throughout Asia and Africa. ❸ Signs of leprosy have been found in ancient Egyptian mummies. ❹ From 1095 to 1272, Christian crusaders from Europe brought the disease home with them after attempting to capture Jerusalem from the Muslims in the Middle East. ❺ Explorers carried leprosy to North and South America in the 1700s. ❻ Leprosy first appeared in the United States and Hawaii in 1758.

they occupied and to bring it home to their own families when they returned to Europe.

Cases of leprosy increased in Europe in the Middle Ages. Although people were still terrified by leprosy, they were more afraid of bubonic plague. The plague was a gruesome and painful disease that killed most of the people it struck within a few days. When outbreaks of the plague decreased in the mid–14th century, there were fewer cases of leprosy. Scientists

Leprosy: A Terrifying Disease **11**

are not sure exactly why this happened. Possibly it was because many lepers were killed by bubonic plague and so could no longer spread the disease. In addition, because so many people died from the plague, living conditions became less crowded and diseases were not spread as easily.

Although the number of people with leprosy was decreasing in Europe, cases were on the rise in other parts of the world. Explorers brought the disease to North and South America in the 1700s. The first outbreak of leprosy in the United States was in Louisiana in 1758. Other outbreaks followed in Texas, Florida, Hawaii, and California. By the mid–20th century, leprosy was not a problem in most developed countries. However, it still thrived in many underdeveloped areas, including India, China, and countries in South America and Africa.

Chapter Two

What Causes Leprosy?

For thousands of years, no one knew what caused leprosy. People knew that a person could get leprosy by getting close to someone who had it, but nobody knew how. It was even more puzzling when a person who had not been near anyone with leprosy would start to show signs of the disease. Scientists know now that once a person has been exposed to leprosy, he or she may not show signs of the disease for up to twenty years. But people in the Middle Ages did not know that, so they came up with other ways to explain why people got leprosy.

Old Ideas

In the *Bible,* God sometimes punishes a person by striking him or her with leprosy. The *Bible* has many references to lepers being "unclean," meaning that they were immoral, sinful, and perhaps even evil. In this *Bible* verse from *Numbers* (12:9–10), Miriam gets leprosy because God is angry with her and her husband: "The anger of the Lord burned against them, and he left them. When the cloud lifted from above the tent, there stood Miriam, leprous."

People in the Middle Ages believed that leprosy was a punishment from God. Most people in Europe were Christians during this time. They believed that people with leprosy were not only sinful, but also quick tempered, crafty, and deceptive. It was commonly thought that lepers were a danger to society not just because they could spread the infection, but also because of their evil behavior.

An Inherited Disease?

By the mid-1800s, some medical scientists thought the disease was inherited, meaning that it was passed down from parents to children. Norwegian physician Daniel Danielssen thought leprosy could be inherited because members of the same family often suffered from the disease. He also noted that people who treated lepers, such as doctors and nurses, often did not get the disease. To prove this point he went as far as to infect himself and some of his colleagues with leprosy. This was done by "making a cut in the skin, filling it with tissue from the leprous node of a patient, and then sewing it up."[1] Although this method was painful, it did not give anyone leprosy. This was

Jesus heals a group of lepers in this *Bible* illustration. The *Bible* often refers to lepers as unclean and sinful people.

probably because, like most of the population, they were immune to the disease.

An Important Discovery

Danielssen's son-in-law Gerhard Henrik Armauer Hansen did not believe that leprosy was inherited. He thought that leprosy was contagious and that it was spread by **bacteria**. He used a microscope to look at tissue samples from people with leprosy for more than a year before he found what he was looking for. In February 1873, Hansen became the first person to see the bacteria that cause leprosy. He

In 1873, Gerhard Henrik Armauer Hansen discovered the bacteria that cause leprosy.

found the rod shaped bacteria in almost every cell in the lesions of people with the disease.

Although he was the first person to identify the bacteria, he could not prove that it was the cause of leprosy. When he first published his findings, most other doctors did not believe that bacteria were the cause of the disease. At this time in history, people did not know that bacteria could cause disease. Hansen was one of the first scientists to make this connection. Hansen tried to prove how bacteria spread leprosy by exposing animals to the bacteria, but none of the animals developed leprosy.

Eventually, scientists discovered how to grow the bacteria in the footpads of mice, and later it was found that nine–banded armadillos could also be infected with the disease. Showing how animals infected with the bacteria contracted leprosy helped to convince people that bacteria could cause leprosy.

After many years and more research, the medical community accepted Hansen's discovery. Leprosy was renamed Hansen's disease in his honor.

The Bacteria

The bacterium that Hansen saw is called *Mycobacterium leprae*. Scientists are not exactly sure how the bacteria are spread from person to person, but most believe that the bacteria travel through the air when someone with untreated leprosy coughs or sneezes.

A researcher at the Carville Leprosy Clinic in Louisiana holds a nine-banded armadillo infected with the disease.

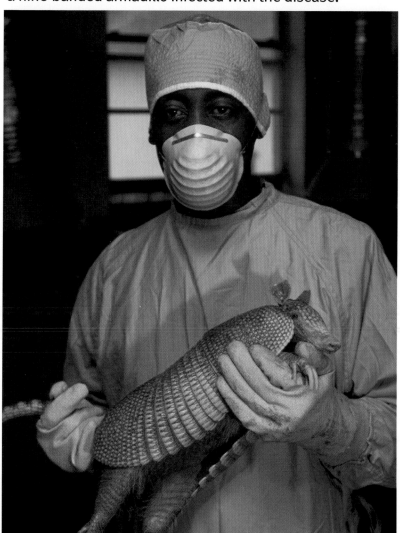

These airborne bacteria may find their way into another body by being inhaled or absorbed through a cut in the skin.

When *Mycobacterium leprae* enters the body, the immune system attacks it with white blood cells. In most cases, the white blood cells will kill the bacteria and the person may not even know of the infection. However, in 5 percent of the people infected, the white blood cells will not be able to kill the bacteria. Scientists do not know why this small group of people cannot fight off the disease. Rather than killing the bacteria, the white blood cells carry it to the cooler parts of the body, such as the hands and

Mycobacterium leprae, the bacteria that cause leprosy, are shown highly magnified under a microscope.

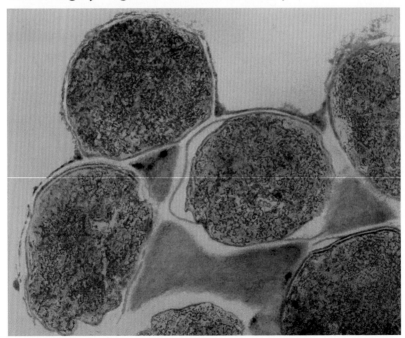

How Scientists Think Leprosy Spreads

① A person with leprosy sneezes or coughs, releasing leprosy bacteria into the air.

② A healthy person might inhale the bacteria, or it may enter through a cut in the skin.

③ White blood cells attack the Bacteria. The attacking cells kill the bacteria in 95 percent of people.

④ In 5 percent of people, the white blood cells are unable to kill the leprosy bacteria.

⑤ In these people, white blood cells carry the bacteria to the hands and feet. There, the bacteria grow very slowly, eventually harming nerves and skin.

feet. There it will continue to grow, damaging the nerves and skin.

Unlike other bacteria, *Mycobacterium leprae* grow very slowly. Bacteria grow by dividing themselves in half. Some bacteria do this every 40 minutes. *Mycobacterium leprae* divide only once every two weeks. Because the bacteria grow so slowly, it takes a long time before a person gets sick. This is why a person who contracts leprosy may not see any sign of the disease for up to eight years, and in some cases, up to twenty years.

Types of Leprosy

Although there is only one kind of bacteria that causes leprosy, there are three kinds of leprosy. The type of leprosy a person gets depends on how his or her body reacts to the bacteria. If the white blood cells are successful at surrounding the bacteria, the symptoms of the disease will be mild. This type of infection is called paucibacillary leprosy. It is the most common type of leprosy. Seventy to eighty percent of people who have leprosy have this type.

When the white blood cells cannot effectively surround the bacteria, the symptoms will be more severe. In multibacillary leprosy, large amounts of the bacteria attack the body. Although this is not as common as paucibacillary leprosy, multibacillary leprosy is more contagious. This is because the bacteria can grow more freely and, therefore, there are more bacteria in the person's body to be spread to other people. Often a patient's symptoms are somewhere in between these two types of leprosy. These patients are classified as having the third type of leprosy: borderline.

The discovery of the bacteria that cause leprosy was an important step toward finding a cure for the disease, but it was important for another reason. When people learned that bacteria caused leprosy, the disease lost some of its stigma. Society stopped blaming people with leprosy for getting the disease and began to treat them with more dignity and respect.

Chapter Three

Living with Leprosy

Until recently, people with leprosy were publicly shamed, neglected, and treated with cruelty. Lepers have rarely been treated kindly, but they probably received the worst treatment in the Middle Ages. When a person was diagnosed with leprosy in the Middle Ages, the priest of the village would cast the leper out of the community, sometimes declaring the person dead. From then on, the person would have to wear special clothing and ring a bell or use a horn to warn of his or her approach. A leper was forbidden to enter any public place, to use the village well or spring, to eat with others, or to use anyone else's eating utensils. He or she was also not allowed to touch or give things to children.

Because lepers were not allowed to work, many of them became beggars. They lived in caves or in

A saint gives charity to lepers in this engraving. During the Middle Ages, most lepers were forced to beg in order to survive.

the forests near the towns. Those with money sometimes lived in hospitals for lepers. In the 1800s, most people with leprosy were put into hospitals or colonies where they spent the remainder of their lives. One of the most famous leper colonies was in Hawaii.

Molokai

In 1865, the government of Hawaii declared that any person diagnosed with leprosy must be banished to Kalaupapa, a peninsula on the island of Molokai. People with leprosy were brought to Kalaupapa by boat and left there. High cliffs prevented them from getting to the rest of the island.

Conditions on the peninsula were appalling. There was not enough to eat because most of the people in the colony were too sick to use the seeds and tools that were left for them. Many died of starvation. Those who survived lived in filthy, poorly constructed huts. There were no doctors, nurses, or medical supplies. Because there were no laws or police, there was a lot of fighting, gambling, drinking, and stealing.

Father Damien

In 1873, Father Damien, a Belgian priest serving in Hawaii, volunteered to help the lepers on Molokai. He did not have leprosy but wanted to help those who did. Damien felt a great compassion for the people in the colony and felt it was his life's work to help them. Damien treated the people of the colony with respect. He settled disputes, bandaged wounds, comforted the dying, and made coffins for the dead. He taught them to plant sweet potatoes, and he cleaned and repaired buildings. Perhaps even more important, he wrote countless letters to the U.S. government asking for supplies, and to newspapers telling of the horrible conditions at the leper colony on Molokai.

The newspapers printed stories about the hardships of people with leprosy at Molokai and people from the other Hawaiian islands began collecting

Father Damien (inset) dedicated his life to helping the colony of lepers that lived on the Hawaiian island of Molokai.

supplies for the colony. Eventually, the government sent medicine, supplies, and a doctor. More buildings were constructed, including churches, hospitals, orphanages, and a school. For sixteen years, Father Damien dedicated his life to the colony but he was not immune to the disease. He continued his work, even as he became sicker. Father Damien died from leprosy on April 15, 1889.

Today Kalaupapa is a national historic park and home to the few patients who choose to live the rest of their lives there.

Carville Hospital

Lepers were also sent to Carville Hospital in Louisiana against their will. Carville was used as a hospital for people with leprosy from 1894 to 1999. A girl with leprosy from Texas named Rachel Pendleton came to Carville in 1944. According to a news report by CNN reporter Charles Zewe, "Pendleton was just 14 when mysterious, numb lumps appeared on her legs. When state health workers came to her home in Corpus Christi, Texas, to take her away, her parents weren't even allowed to hug her good-bye."[2] People with leprosy were sent to Carville from all over the United States.

Patients at Carville Hospital in Louisiana, seen here in 1955, were often treated like prisoners.

For many years, residents felt Carville was more like a prison than a hospital. For example, when the hospital first began to take patients, male and female residents were separated by a wall and forbidden to marry. The staff was discouraged from mingling with the patients, and patients were cut off from the outside world. The fence that surrounded the hospital was topped with barbed wire and the long road leading to it was unpaved. There was no post office and no phone for the residents. Patients could not vote, and visits from friends and family were limited. Occasionally patients were allowed to take short vacations to visit their families, but only if they did not use public transportation.

One Man's Impact

In 1931, a man named Stanley Stein was admitted to Carville. He was upset by the rules and the fact that no one was doing anything to improve the situation. "It was the curious feeling of hopeless apathy I encountered everywhere that so depressed me [and a lack of] desire to work for the common good,"[3] said Stein. Stein started a newspaper called *The Star* to be distributed within the hospital and to the community outside. In it, he included interesting articles about activities and residents. He also wrote articles that called for change within the hospital and tried to educate people about leprosy.

In the fourth issue of *The Star,* Dr. Guy Faget, head medical officer at Carville, wrote an article called

"Courage" in which he tried to take away the shame that had always been associated with leprosy. "This is the modern age, the age of light," he wrote. "Let us have the truth. Leprosy is not a dirt disease. Leprosy is not due to any sin committed by those who contract it. It is not a retaliation of God against its victims. Leprosy is a germ disease. . . . It is no more shameful to be inflicted with the germs of leprosy than with those of tuberculosis, typhoid or pneumonia."[4]

Thanks to the efforts of Stanley Stein, this Carville patient was discharged from the facility and led a normal life.

A man and his mother, both suffering from leprosy, look for charity on the streets of Calcutta, India.

The Star played a major role in changing life at Carville. Gradually, people began to understand that leprosy was not contagious to most people and that people with leprosy were not to blame for their disease. In the 1950s, residents of Carville had more contact with the outside world. By this time a cure had been found for leprosy. Rather than staying at Carville for many years or even a lifetime, people came for a few months, were treated and cured, and then returned home. Some people chose to stay because the disease had left them permanently disfigured. Those who stayed could marry, have visitors, own cars, and lead somewhat normal lives. Because of people like Stein, lepers are no longer treated as outcasts in developed countries. However, this is not so in many developing countries like India.

Leprosy in India

In many parts of India, people with leprosy are still treated cruelly. There are people in India who do not understand that bacteria cause leprosy. Some of them still believe that people get leprosy because they have done bad things in a previous life. Because of such beliefs, there are people in India who hide the fact that they have leprosy because they fear becoming outcasts. This is what happened to Nudin Culhea.

Nudin Culhea saw the first signs of leprosy when he was just seven years old. He hid the disease from his family for several years. When his family discovered that he had leprosy they made him leave. Because he did not get treatment, his hands and feet became badly twisted. "I tried to commit suicide" he says, "but it didn't work. I have nothing, no one. I'll never get married."[5] If Nudin had been treated when he first got the disease, he could have lived a normal life.

The outlook for many people with leprosy living in India is not promising. Most who have suffered from severe leprosy cannot work because they are blind or unable to use their hands and feet. But even if they are not disabled, those who are disfigured from leprosy still have trouble getting hired. Forced to become beggars, they may live on a diet of rice and water and have no money for bandages and clothing. They may be homeless, living on the street, or in colonies with other people who have leprosy. Most of these colonies are slums without electricity, freshwater, or sewer systems.

Helping people in India who have leprosy is a big job. Although leprosy can be cured, there are many people who no longer have the disease but are still severely disfigured. These people often live in colonies where charitable organizations, such as LEPRA (Leprosy Relief Association), are devoted to helping them. Groups such as LEPRA offer treatment, bandages, and food. They improve the sanitation in colonies, build wells, and teach people to grow food. Such improvements not only make life better for people who have been disfigured by leprosy, but they also help them to regain their dignity and to feel they have a place in society.

Chapter Four

Leprosy Today

Until the mid–20th century, there was no effective cure for leprosy. Patients were sometimes treated with chaulmoogra, which is a thick oil with a bad smell. But the treatment lasted for many years, was painful, and not very effective. In the 1940s, Dr. Guy Faget of the Carville Hospital found that the antibiotic dapsone was effective against leprosy. This drug saved people from a life of isolation and disfigurement and helped to take away some of the stigma of the disease. Eventually other effective drugs were discovered.

Treatment for Leprosy

Today leprosy is treated using a treatment program called **multidrug therapy (MDT)**. A combination of three different antibiotics is used to combat the

Although these antileprosy drugs cure leprosy, they cannot reverse any damage the disease has caused.

disease. When taken together, they kill the bacteria that cause leprosy, curing the disease. These drugs are highly effective, and once the disease is gone, it does not return. Although the treatment period is long—six to twelve months—patients are no longer contagious after the first dose. For most patients, these drugs cause only minor side effects.

These drugs cure leprosy, but they cannot fix the damaging effects that years of leprosy have on the body. People who have had leprosy for many years are left with disfigured hands, feet, and faces and serious nerve damage.

Continuing Challenges

There are many programs to help people who have had leprosy deal with the effects of the disease. The most effective strategies are community-based **rehabilitation** programs. These programs help people with leprosy in a variety of ways.

Education is a big part of rehabilitation. People who have nerve damage must learn to take good care of themselves. Because they have lost the sense of touch in some parts of their bodies, they do not know when they have been injured. When wounds are left unattended, they can turn into dangerous

A cured leprosy patient teaches children in a village in Senegal. The village was founded in 1914 to isolate lepers, but today all of them have been cured.

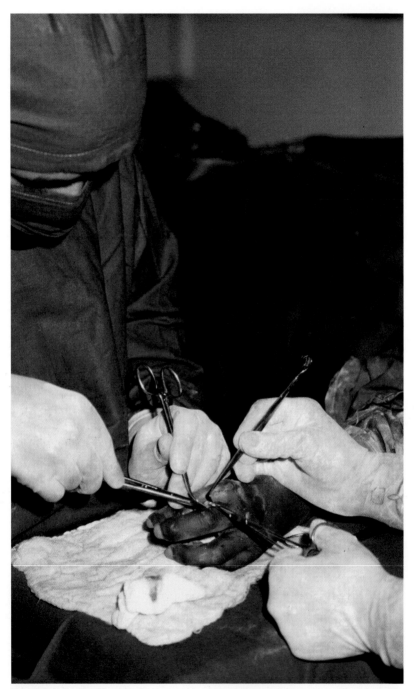

Doctors in India perform reconstructive surgery on the hand of a leprosy patient in an effort to correct his deformities.

infections. Wearing shoes and protective clothing is one way to prevent injury. Some people with deformed feet may need special shoes. It is important to teach people who have lost the sensation in their hands or feet to constantly check for bruises, cuts, and other injuries and attend to them immediately.

People with nerve damage can also benefit from therapeutic exercises to keep the deformities from getting worse. Such exercises can also help them to increase their ability to move their hands and feet. In many cases, splints and braces can also be used to correct some of the damage caused by leprosy.

Sometimes reconstructive surgery can be used to treat a deformity. Some of the more common surgeries help correct deformities in the hands and feet. Surgery may also be used to reconstruct a nose or other part of the face, such as the eyes, for people who can no longer close their eyes.

Education

Many organizations teach skills to people disabled by leprosy so that they can earn money and support themselves. Efforts to teach recovered leprosy patients skills like farming, auto repair, carpentry, pottery, and sewing have been very successful. Some organizations even help people disabled by leprosy to start their own businesses by loaning them small sums of money. Often these organizations offer counseling to help people deal with their disabilities. The focus on education, effective treatments, and rehabilitation programs has played a major role in the battle against leprosy.

Winning the Battle

The battle against leprosy has been a very successful one. In most countries, leprosy is rare. In the United States, about 100 people a year are diagnosed with the disease. Most of these people are immigrants or refugees who got the disease in another country before coming to the United States. In 1985, over 15 million people had leprosy. Today that number is down to half a million. Ninety percent of all leprosy cases occur in just six countries: India, Brazil, Madagascar, Mozambique, Myanmar, and Nepal.

The World Health Organization (WHO) has played a major role in the battle against leprosy. In 1991, WHO launched its Final Push program to eliminate leprosy worldwide. But eliminating the disease does not mean that it will go away and never return. WHO defined elimination as no more than 1 person being diagnosed with the disease in every 10,000 people. Originally, WHO thought leprosy could be eliminated by the year 2000. Although great progress was made, leprosy was not eliminated in all parts of the world by this date, so the program was extended to 2005. Even as the number of people who get leprosy dramatically decreases, there will probably always be some new cases, because the bacteria still exist.

There are several reasons why the number of cases of leprosy has dramatically decreased. Gov-

At a hospital in the Philippines, a leprosy patient learns to sew so that she can support herself in the outside world.

ernments, charitable organizations, and WHO have worked together in the fight against leprosy. They have worked to remove the stigma associated with leprosy by educating people about the disease. Today, most people who get leprosy are more likely to seek treatment early because they are not afraid of being mistreated and are not ashamed of having the disease. Also, the drugs needed to cure leprosy are now available free of charge all around the world. This has resulted in many people with leprosy getting treatment before the disease causes permanent damage.

Education and free treatment made a huge difference to Arifin, a boy living in Indonesia. A Mr. Sudarmaji from the local health center came to talk at his school about leprosy. Mr. Sudarmaji showed the children pictures of what leprosy looks like in the beginning stages and made sure that everyone understood how important it was to get help right away. A few years later, Arifin developed patches that looked like the ones from the pictures. "I had a

In Madagascar, a reporter visits with children being treated for leprosy. Madagascar is one of six countries where the majority of leprosy cases occur today.

choice," Arifin said. "I could be quiet and try to ignore it, and not tell anyone, because it would be very embarrassing to have people know that I had leprosy. My friends might stay away from me, people maybe would think I was bad or dirty. But I remembered that Mr. Sudarmaji had pleaded with us not to wait; because our nerves could be damaged."[6] Arifin told his parents and they brought him to the health center where he received the drugs he needed to cure the disease. Today, Arifin is a healthy boy of seventeen with no nerve damage and no deformities.

Future Outlook

Although the leprosy bacterium has not gone away, it causes far less damage than it did in years past. As more and more people receive treatment early, the damage and disfigurement are becoming things of the past. Leper colonies and forced isolation have also become less common. Rajesh, a young man from India, is an example of how much progress has been made. According to LEPRA, "Rajesh was diagnosed as suffering from leprosy. He was thrown out of his home as well as the village where he lived. He was found by a LEPRA Paramedical Worker and put on a course of multidrug therapy. The Paramedical Worker then arranged a village meeting, inviting the whole village as well as the leaders to ask them to accept Rajesh back into the community. His uncle came forward and offered to let Rajesh come and live with him."[7] Rajesh returned to his village

This young leprosy patient in Indonesia was able to seek medical attention before the disease caused any permanent damage.

and, with the help of a government loan, started a successful business raising cows to sell at the market.

Rajesh's story is not unusual. Other similar stories can be found throughout India and in other underdeveloped countries where leprosy has been a problem. Many health care professionals consider the fight against leprosy to be one of the biggest public health success stories in history.

Notes

Chapter 2: What Causes Leprosy?

1. "Who Named It," Daniel Cornelius Danielssen. www.whonamedit.com/doctor.cfm/2321.html.

Chapter 3: Living with Leprosy

2. Charles Zewe, "Leprosy hospital's closure means new start for patients," CNN, April 24, 1998. www.cnn.com/US/9804/24/last.lepers.
3. Quoted in Amy L. Fairchild, *Community and Confinement: The Evolving Experience of Isolation for Leprosy in Carville, Louisiana.* Public Health Reports, May/June 2004, p. 362.
4. G.H. Faget, "Courage," *Star,* December 1941, p. 3.
5. Quoted in Jonathon Harley, "India Fights Leprosy Legacy," *World Today,* May 15, 2000. www.abc.net.au/worldtoday/stories/s126859.htm.

Chapter 4: Leprosy Today

6. Quoted in The Leprosy Mission, "Leprosy Without Disability, Arifin's Story." www.tlmtrading.com index.cfm?section=news&action=view&id=66.
7. LEPRA, "Patient Stories from India: Rajesh." www.lepra.org.uk/projects/india_patients.html.

Glossary

amputated: A limb removed in a surgical operation.

bacteria: One-celled organisms that can cause disease.

contagious: Capable of being spread from one person to another by direct or indirect contact.

deformities: Parts of the body that have formed abnormally.

disfiguring: Marred or malformed.

gangrene: The decay of a part of a person's body.

lesions: Areas in or on the body that have suffered damage through injury or disease.

multi-drug therapy (MDT): A combination of different drugs given to a patient to cure a disease.

numbness: A lack of physical sensation.

paralyzed: Unable to move a part of the body as a result of damage to nerve or muscle function.

rehabilitation: Training, therapy, or other help given to somebody to return them to health after an illness or injury.

stigma: The shame or disgrace associated with something regarded as socially unacceptable.

For Further Exploration

Books

Beverly Birch, *Father Damien, Missionary to the Forgotten People.* Milwaukee WI: G Stevens Books, 1990. In this book, the author has adapted Pam Brown's biography of Father Damien for younger readers. Includes pictures and maps.

Karen Donnely, *Leprosy (Hansen's Disease).* New York: Rosen, 2002. This book includes information about the history of leprosy, what causes the disease, and how it is treated. Includes interesting photographs, a time line, and a glossary.

Brain R. Ward, *Epidemic.* New York: Dorling Kindersley, in association with the American Museum of Natural History, 2000. Part of the DK Eyewitness series, this colorful book explains how epidemics such as malaria start and spread.

Web Sites

BBC News: In Pictures: Raising the Awareness of Leprosy (news.bbc.co.uk/1/hi/in_depth/photo _gallery/3401031.stm). This site features eight graphic pictures of people who have been affected by leprosy.

CDC Disease Information: Hansen's Disease (Leprosy) (www.cdc.gov/ncidod/dbmd/disease info/hansens_t.htm). This site from the Centers for Disease Control and Prevention outlines the facts about leprosy.

Kalaupapa National Historical Park, Molokai, Hawaii (www.arizonamemorial.org/kalaupapa. html). The official site of the historical park, which commemorates the Kalaupapa leper colony. Includes information about the colony and leprosy, as well as information about how to visit the park.

Patient Stories from India (www.lepra.org.uk/ projects/india_patients.htm). This page features some stories from the LEPRA Web site about people in India who have had leprosy.

The Star (www.thestar.info/directory.htm). This site features information about Carville Hospital and its residents, including original issues of *The Star* from the 1940s.

Index

45

Picture Credits

About the Author

Rachel Lynette has written several other books for KidHaven Press, as well as dozens of articles on children and family life. She also teaches science to children of all ages. Rachel lives in the Seattle area in the Songaia Cohousing Community with her two children David and Lucy, her dog Jody, and two playful rats. When she is not teaching or writing, she enjoys spending time with her family and friends, traveling, reading, drawing, in-line skating, and eating chocolate ice cream.